Matthew | 1 Thessalonians | Genesis

24 studies for Bible-reading partnerships

Andrew Cornes

For all those with whom I have enjoyed Bible-reading partnerships down the years and who have helped me to understand, apply and delight in the Bible's teaching.

One2One Book 2

The Good Book Company
Elm House, 37 Elm Road
New Malden, Surrey KT3 3HB
Tel (UK): 0845 225 0880
Tel (int): +(44) 208 942 0880
email: admin@thegoodbook.co.uk
Websites:
UK & Europe: www.thegoodbook.co.uk
N America: www.thegoodbook.com
Australia: www.thegoodbook.com.au
New Zealand: www.thegoodbook.co.nz

ISBN: 9781906334956

Printed in India

Introduction Why read the Bible together?

"Two are better than one, because they have a good reward for their toil" ECCLESIASTES 4 v 9

These words were originally written for a work context: it is better to work with someone else than to work alone. The wisdom books of the Bible (Proverbs, Ecclesiastes, Job, Song of Solomon) have a great deal to say about partnership and friendship.

For many Christians reading the Bible is hard work. We manage it for a time and then we give up. Or we keep going without getting much out of our reading. There can be great gain in meeting regularly to read the Bible with one other person: a friend or our marriage partner.

A Bible-reading partnership can revitalise our reading of the Bible: bringing new insights and keeping us up to the mark. We may well discover that our reading alone also becomes easier. And it all began when we discovered *ONE2ONE*.

1. **AIM:** The aim is that two Christians should encourage each other as they meet regularly to read God's word and talk about what it says. Bible-reading partnerships are no substitute for personal Bible study (except on the day you meet!). At their best, they inspire us to read the Bible more at other times.

2. **PARTNER:** Choose your Bible-reading partner carefully. If you are married, you may want to have your husband/wife as your Bible-reading partner. Otherwise we strongly advise that you choose a partner of your own sex. It can be good if a more experienced Christian reads with a person who knows their Bible less well.

3. **FREQUENCY:** The ideal is to meet weekly. Some find that it is better for them to meet every other week. We do not advise meeting less frequently than every other week, if at all possible.

4. **TIMING:** We suggest that you set aside 90 minutes and keep strictly

to whatever timing you have agreed. It is normally a good idea to begin the Bible study as soon as possible after arrival, and to catch up on news at the end rather than the beginning; experience shows that otherwise the time of Bible study gets squeezed. One suggestion is: Bible study 45-60 minutes; praying together 5-15 minutes.

5 **STUDYING THE BIBLE:** There are 24 sessions: a passage for each session and questions on it. The aim of these questions is the same as in all genuine study of the Bible: to help us...
• understand what the Bible writer was saying; and
• apply that message to our lives today.

You will not always be able to discuss all the questions. That is fine; but make sure you always discuss some of those questions which make you apply the passage to your life today.

6 **PREPARATION:** You will get most out of the partnership if you study the passage carefully before you meet, and note down your answers to the questions. This will undoubtedly make your discussion richer. It is, however, possible to benefit from the Bible-reading partnership without studying the passage in advance.

7 **VERSION OF THE BIBLE:** The questions occasionally quote from the English Standard Version of the Bible. It is perfectly possible, however, to answer the questions using any other good modern translation.

8 **ORDER:** The 24 sessions are designed to be studied in the following order: Matthew 26 – 28 (sessions 1-8); 1 Thessalonians (sessions 9-16); Genesis 1 – 12 (sessions 17-24). This probably provides the best progression. If, however, you wish to go through the sessions in a different order, that is fine.

9 **PRAYING:** It is always good practice to pray before we read a passage from the Bible. We want God to speak to us; and it is obvious that we need to ask Him to do so.

In addition, there are suggestions for *Praying Together* at the end of each session. When God has spoken to us, we need to speak in response to Him. These suggestions frequently say: "Pray for each other". Having discussed and shared together, it is a great encouragement to hear someone else pray about our thoughts/ concerns, rather than each of us praying about what we ourselves have mentioned.

As you get to know each other better, it will be very natural, of course, to pray about other concerns not directly related to the Bible study. We suggest that you pray home the truths of the passage you have just been reading before you pray for other concerns/needs. Otherwise, you and your partner's immediate, pressing needs can edge out the eternal truth you have just been hearing from God.

10 **REVIEW SHEETS:** At the end of each group of sessions there is a review sheet. Please complete this before going on to the next group of sessions. It will help consolidate what you have learned from the Bible. If there is someone in your church in charge of Bible-reading partnerships, please make a photocopy of each review sheet and send or give this to him/her.

11 **STARTING AGAIN:** At the end of the course, we hope that you will be able to start again with a new Bible-reading partner. Your experience will be invaluable to your new partner. In this way, more and more Christians will have the benefits of being involved in a Bible-reading partnership.

12 **IF IT DOESN'T WORK OUT:** Sometimes a Bible-reading partnership doesn't fully work. Occasionally the partners don't gel or one partner has to drop out. This is often nobody's fault. We would encourage you to choose a new partner; this new partnership will very likely go well.

13 **FURTHER READING:** Some people have asked for reading suggestions to help with these studies. This is not necessary but it can be helpful (as long as you don't make your Bible-reading partner feel small because they haven't done any extra reading). Over the page are some suggestions: in each case, the first book is slimmer and the second a little more detailed.

MATTHEW 26 – 28
- M. Green, *The Message of Matthew,* IVP
- R. T. France, *Matthew*, IVP

1 THESSALONIANS
- W. Barclay, *Philippians, Colossians and Thessalonians*, St. Andrews Press
- J. R. W. Stott, *The Message of Thessalonians*, IVP

GENESIS 1-12
- D. Atkinson, *The Message of Genesis 1-11*, IVP
- D. Kidner, *Genesis*, IVP

Matthew 26 – 28

Learning from Matthew's account of Jesus' trial, death and rising again

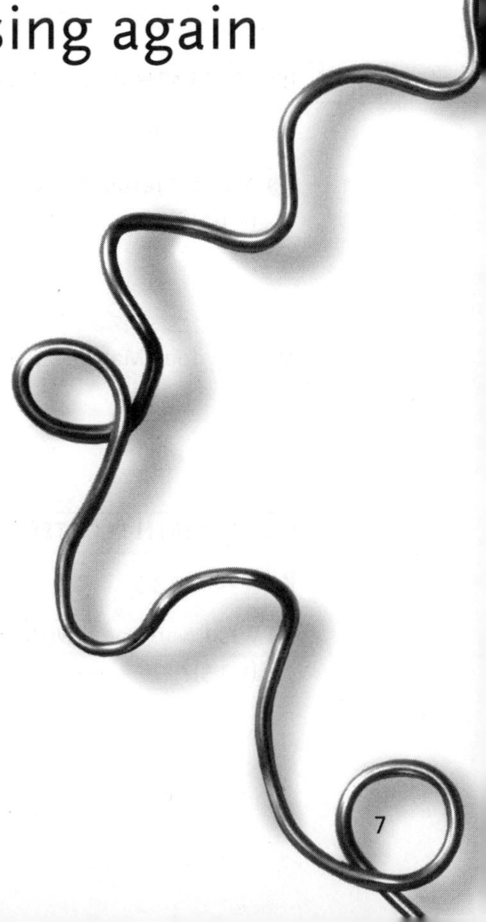

Session 1

Why it happened
and why we're told it happened

Today's passage: **Matthew 26 v 1-16**

The Gospels put us in touch with two periods: the time of Jesus and the time of the Gospel writer. God can teach us truths both from what Jesus said and did and from how the Gospel writer explains the story, and why he includes it in his book. When reading the Gospels, it is good to get into the habit of regularly asking 2 questions:

- Why did Jesus say this (or do that)?
- Why did Matthew (or another Gospel writer) choose to include this story?

The same applies to any narrative [= history] part of the Bible. We can, for example, ask both "Why did David act with such courage towards Goliath?" and "Why did the writer of 1 Samuel choose to include this story?"

A JESUS' DEATH PREDICTED

Read verses 1-2

1. Why did Jesus tell His disciples in advance about His crucifixion (v 1-2)?

2. Why does Matthew tell us in advance about Jesus' crucifixion (v 1-2)?

B JESUS' DEATH PLOTTED

Read verses 3-5

3. What were the Jewish authorities afraid of in Jesus and in the people (v 3-5)?

❹ Why does Matthew tell us this straight after Jesus' prediction (v 1-5)? What's the irony?

C JESUS' DEATH PREPARED FOR

Read verses 6-13

❺ In what ways was the woman's act not a waste (v 6-13)?

❻ In what way(s) does the woman "prepare Jesus for burial" (v 12)?

❼ Why does Matthew include this story in the Passion narrative (v 6-13)?

❽ What extravagant thing might God be asking you to do for Jesus (v 6-13)?

D JESUS' DEATH PAID FOR

Read verses 14-16

❾ What do these verses tell us about how tragic Judas' betrayal is (v 14-16)?

❿ Why does Matthew include this story straight after the woman and her ointment (v 6-16)?

E PRAYING TOGETHER

- Praise Jesus for what you have seen of His authority and character in this passage.
- Pray for your Bible-reading partner that (s)he will serve Jesus extravagantly, especially in any way (s)he may have mentioned in answer to question 8.

Session 2 Listening to Jesus at Passover

Today's passage: Matthew 26 v 17-30

There are two dangers in reading parts of the Bible with which we are very familiar, like Matthew 26 – 28: one is to read quickly and superficially, thinking we know the story already; the other is to read into the Bible account more than is actually there. It is always worth asking:

- What are the parts of his account which the writer thought were most important?
- What did he mean us to learn from them?

A THE PASSOVER MEAL: BETRAYAL PREDICTED

Read verses 17-25

1. In verses 17-19, what is the most striking thing that Jesus says? What does it tell us about Jesus?

2. What did Jesus want His disciples to learn as He spoke about His betrayal (v 20-25)?

3. What did Jesus want Judas to learn as He (Jesus) spoke about His betrayal (v 20-25)?

❹ What betrayals of Jesus should make us "very sorrowful" (v 22)?

B THE PASSOVER MEAL: BREAD AND WINE REINTERPRETED

Read verses 26-30

❺ How is the bread of the Last Supper a picture of Christ's body (v 26)?

❻ What do Christ's words about the cup tell us about His death (v 27-28)?

❼ Jesus' "drink[ing] it new with you in my Father's kingdom" probably means: at the end of time (see 8 v 11; 25 v 10). Is Jesus giving the disciples bad news or good news in verse 29? Why?

❽ How will this passage's teaching enrich the next time you take Communion / the Lord's Supper?

C PRAYING TOGETHER

- Pray for those (perhaps including yourself) who have betrayed Jesus.
- Pray for your Bible-reading partner's response to Jesus as (s)he next shares in Communion / the Lord's Supper, especially in the light of your answers to question 8.

Session 3 Concentrating on Jesus

Today's passage: Matthew 26 v 30-56

The Gospel writers wrote their Passion narratives principally to tell us about Jesus. But we prefer to think about ourselves: when, for example, we read about Jesus' praying in Gethsemane (v 36-46), we tend to ask what lessons we can learn for our own prayer. This is of course not wrong, but the Gospel writers tell us about these last days of Jesus' life on earth primarily to draw out our faith and love and worship, rather than to present Jesus as our example. We should often be asking: What glories in Jesus does each passage show me?

A JESUS' PREDICTION

Read verses 30-35

1. Are Jesus' words in v 31-32 a rebuke or an encouragement? Why?

2. When you hear that people will "fall away" (v 31, 33), do you react like Peter, or not? Why/Why not (v 31-35)?

B JESUS' PRAYER

Read verses 36-46

3. Since Jesus knew exactly what was going to happen (v 1-2), why did He need to spend the night praying (v 36-46)?

4. Why did Jesus so much want the three disciples to pray (v 36-46)?

5 How did God change Jesus' attitude as He continued to pray (v 37-46)?

6 How does this account of the time in Gethsemane before the arrest enrich your respect and love for Jesus (v 36-46)?

C JESUS' ARREST

Read verses 47-56

7 Since Jesus could have stopped His arrest at any time (v 53; see also John 18 v 4-6), why did He let it happen (v 47-56)? What are the clues in the passage (v 47-56)?

8 Looking back over the passage as a whole (v 30-56), what is your overriding impression of Jesus on that night? What gives you that impression (v 30-56)?

D PRAYING TOGETHER

- Begin with some silence, to think back over the events in Jesus' life you've just been studying. If it helps, imagine each scene in your mind, as if you were present; or take a pencil and draw the scene.
- Take time to praise Jesus together for the beautiful and glorious aspects of His character you have seen. If you can, pray several prayers, not just one each.

Session 4 Jesus' opponents—then and now

Today's passage: Matthew 26 v 57-68

In this passage the focus is (almost) as much on Jesus' opponents as on Jesus Himself. So while we will continue to ask what His trial before Caiaphas shows us about Jesus, we will also be asking if (and how) present-day opponents of Christ mirror the attitudes of the Jewish Supreme Council.

A THE TRIAL: INITIAL STAGES

Read verses 57-63a

1. What does Matthew want us to think about the trial of Jesus (v 57-63a)? Why does he believe we need to know this?

2. Jesus did say something like v 61 (see John 2 v 18-22); why didn't He answer the charge (v 60-63a)?

B THE TRIAL: THE CRUNCH

Read verses 63b-66

3. When Jesus is asked directly who He is, He gives a very explicit answer. What exactly does He tell Caiaphas, and us, about Himself (v 63b-64)?

4 What did Caiaphas find so offensive in Jesus' answer (v 64-66)? Do people find the same truths offensive today (v 64-66)? Why?

C THE TRIAL: THE AFTERMATH

Read verses 67-68

5 The Gospel writers are very sparing in their description of the pain of the cross. Why does Matthew tell us what Christ suffered in v 67-68?

6 Put yourself (if you can) in Christ's shoes. What may/must have been going through His mind during and after His trial (v 57-68)?

7 What people in power today abuse and lie about Christ (v 57-68)? How does this passage help us to come to terms with that (v 57-68)?

D PRAYING TOGETHER

- Give praise to Jesus for all that He went through for us in His trial.
- Pray for those situations today in which Christ and His people are abused. Be guided in how you pray by your answers to both questions under question 7.

Session 5 What's it there for?

Today's passage: Matthew 26 v 69 – 27 v 10

The Gospel writers tell us no more than they believe we need to know; in many ways their writing is very compact. So a natural question to ask is: Why has the writer included this section? We are very familiar with the stories of Peter's denial and Judas' suicide; but in fact they slow the story down and take the focus away from Jesus, who is not personally present in 26 v 69 – 27 v 10. All the more reason for asking what Matthew was wanting to teach us.

A PETER

Read 26 v 69-75

1. Peter had been so adamant that he would never deny Jesus (v 33-35). Why did he do it to some "servant girls" and "bystanders" (v 58, 69-75)?

2. Is there any progression/change in the ways Peter denies Jesus (v 69-75)? If so, why?

3. What does Matthew want us to learn from this story (v 69-75)?

4. When have you recently denied Christ? And what led to it?

B JUDAS

Read 27 v 1-5

5. How does Matthew want us to react to Judas (v 1-5)? What in the passage shows you this (v 1-5)?

6. Peter "wept bitterly" after his betrayal of Jesus (26 v 75); Judas hanged himself after his (27 v 5). Why the difference?

7. How do you react when you let Christ down? Why?

C THE CHIEF PRIESTS

Read 27 v 6-10

8. What does Matthew want us to think about the chief priests' reaction to the "blood money" (v 6-10)?

9. This whole passage interrupts the story of Jesus, who does not appear in it. Why does Matthew think it's important for us (26 v 69 – 27 v 10)?

D PRAYING TOGETHER

- You may be able to talk with your Bible-reading partner about ways in which you've let Christ down, or that may be too painful and private. Confess these things to Christ, either aloud (see James 5 v 16) or silently.
- Pray together about what you have learned from the passage, in line with your answers to question 9.

Session 6 Silent and passive but centre stage

Today's passage: Matthew 27 v 11-31

One of the features of all the Gospels' accounts of the trial before Pilate (especially in Matthew, Mark and Luke) is that Jesus is silent and passive. In some parts He is not even obviously present (v 15-25). Yet all Matthew's concentration, and ours, is on Him. Matthew has much to teach us about Jesus, even when He is apparently saying or doing nothing.

A THE SILENCE OF JESUS

Read verses 11-14

1. In the trial before Pilate, Matthew only tells us one thing which Jesus said (v 11: "'You have said so" is a slightly guarded/qualified way of saying "yes"); for the rest, Jesus is silent (v 12, 14). What does Matthew want us to make of this (v 11-14)?

B JESUS OR BARABBAS?

Read verses 15-23

2. Pilate presents the crowd with a choice: Jesus or Barabbas; and the crowd respond. Why does Matthew tell us this at some length (v 15-23)?

3. Why does Matthew tell us about Pilate's wife's dream (v 19)?

4. In what ways, if any, are we like Barabbas (v 15-23)?

C GUILTY OF HIS BLOOD

Read verses 24-26

❺ Pilate wants to relinquish responsibility for "this man's blood". What does Matthew want us to make of that (v 24-26)?

❻ The crowd wants to take on responsibility for Jesus' blood. What does Matthew want us to make of that (v 25)?

D MOCKING THE KING

Read verses 27-31

❼ If this had happened to you, which of the elements of the soldiers' mockery would have been most hard to bear (v 27-31)? Why?

❽ Why does Matthew tell us in such detail about the soldiers' mockery (v 27-31)?

❾ With what thoughts and emotions does this whole passage leave you (v 11-31)? Which verses especially give you those reactions?

E PRAYING TOGETHER

- If Jesus is the centre of this passage, let Him also be the centre of your prayers...
- Give praise together for what you've learned about Jesus.
- Bring to Jesus the thoughts and feelings about Him which this passage has evoked in you and which you have talked about in answer to question 9.

Session 7 The death of Jesus

Today's passage: Matthew 27 v 32-54

Mark tells us that Jesus hung on the cross for six hours: from 9am ("the third hour") to 3pm ("the ninth hour") (Mark 15 v 25, 33-34). Clearly many things happened during those six hours, and each Gospel writer chooses carefully what he wants us to know. It is both possible, and legitimate, to put all the accounts together and get a fuller picture: for example, the loud cry (v 50) may well have been Luke 23 v 46 or John 19 v 30. But Matthew chooses not to tell us what words, if any, Jesus used in the cry he mentions. There is a lot to be said for taking each Gospel account separately and asking: What does this inspired writer want us to learn?

This is a longer study with more questions than usual. You may need to miss some questions out or spend two sessions over this study.

A THE FIRST THREE HOURS: WHAT THEY DID TO JESUS

Read verses 32-44

1. Why did Jesus refuse the wine (v 33-34)?

2. What does Matthew want us to think about what the guards did (v 35-36)?

3. What does Matthew want us to think about the charge (= accusation) against Jesus (v 37)?

4. What does Matthew want us to think about what the onlookers said (v 38-44)?

B THE SECOND THREE HOURS: WHAT HAPPENED WHEN JESUS DIED

Read verses 45-50

5. Why does Matthew tell us about the darkness (v 45)? What does it mean?

6. Did Jesus lose His nerve on the cross (v 46; it may be useful to know that v 46 is a quotation of Psalm 22 v 1; and you may find it helpful to read that whole psalm)? What was He saying to God (v 46)?

7. Why does Matthew tell us about the people's misunderstanding (v 47-49)?

8. What does Matthew want us to understand about Jesus' actual dying (v 50)?

C THE AFTERMATH: WHAT RESULTED FROM JESUS' DEATH

Read verses 51-54

9. What does the temple curtain's tearing tell us about the result of Christ's death (v 51)? (Note: This is the curtain which barred entry into the inner sanctuary, where God was present and into which even the high priest could not normally go: see Leviticus 16 v 2.)

10. What do the earthquake and the opening of the tombs tell us about the result of Christ's death (v 51-53)?

11. What are we to make of the centurion's reaction (v 54)?

D PRAYING TOGETHER

- Praise God for new insights that He has given you into Jesus' death.
- Praise Jesus for what He went through for us.

Session 8 Jesus, risen from the dead: the facts and the commands

Today's passage: Matthew 28 v 1-20

No understanding of Christ and His life is complete without the resurrection. Matthew gives us historical facts to show that it took place and tells us about an attempt to discredit it. He also tells us what the risen Jesus expects of His followers. As we study Matthew's final chapter, we need to think how we can explain this historical event to our friends who are interested in the Christian faith but not yet convinced. And we need to think how we can obey Christ's last words to His disciples and to us.

A THE FACTS ON THE GROUND

Read verses 27 v 57 – 28 v 10

1. What facts and experiences convinced the women that Jesus was alive (27 v 59-61 and 28 v 1-10)?

2. What evidence would you bring from this passage to help convince an interested friend that Jesus is alive (v 1-10)?

B THE ALTERNATIVE EXPLANATION

Read verses 11-15

3. Why did the chief priests choose this false story (27 v 62-66 and 28 v 11-15)?

4. What could they not deny (v 11-13)?

5. Were they successful in their ploy (v 15-20)?

C THE LAST WORDS

Read verses 16-20

6. What final message(s) does Jesus want to leave with His disciples (v 16-20)? What is new/revolutionary in this teaching (v 16-20)?

7. What can you do this week to obey what Jesus is saying (v 16-20)?

D PRAYING TOGETHER

- Praise God for what this passage has taught you about how He raised His Son from the dead.
- Pray for each other that you will "go and make disciples" this week and in the months ahead, incorporating your answers to question 7.

Review sheet | Matthew 26 –28

The purposes of this review sheet are:
- to help you evaluate your times together
- to make any changes in these times that would make them more helpful
- to consolidate the lessons God has taught you

Discuss your review with your Bible-reading partner when you next meet.

If there is someone in your church in charge of Bible-reading partnerships, make a photocopy of this review and send or give this copy to him/her.

- *How frequently have you normally met?*

Weekly ❑ Every other week ❑ Once a month ❑ Other ❑

- *Do you want to meet more frequently?*
- *How long did you normally spend?*

Altogether ________ mins In Bible study ________ mins
In prayer ________ mins In general talking ________ mins

- *Do you want to change the balance of your time together?*

- *Which sessions on Matthew 26 – 28 did you find most helpful? Why?*

- *In what ways, if any, have you changed in your understanding of Jesus, or your response to Him, as a result of studying Matthew 26 – 28?*

- *In what ways has your partner helped you as you have read the Bible and prayed together?*

1 Thessalonians

Hearing God’s word to the Thessalonians and then to us

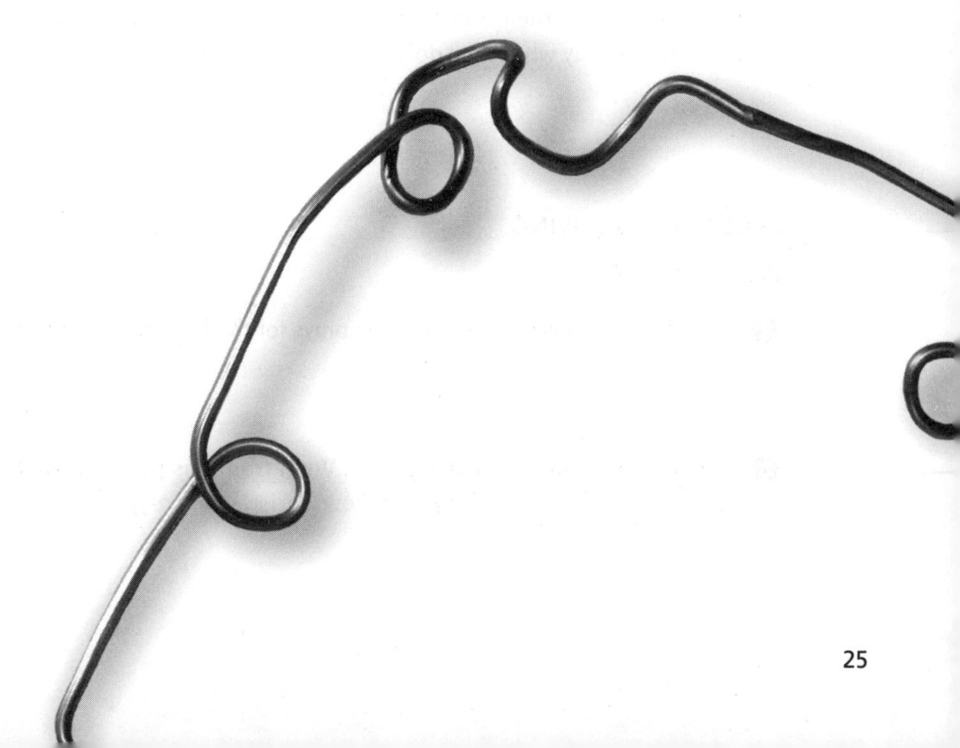

Session 9 First to the Thessalonians – then to us

Today's passage: 1 Thessalonians 1 v 1-10

Much of the New Testament consists of letters from Paul (or some other Christian leader) to churches or individuals. It is natural for us to put ourselves in the shoes of the people who received the letter, so that God's word comes not only to the Thessalonians but, through what Paul says to them, also to us. It is also often appropriate to want to be like the writer of the letter: in this case, like Paul (see 2 Thessalonians 3 v 9). Certainly the New Testament letters will only have their God-intended effect if we first hear what the original writer said to the original recipients, and then apply those same truths to ourselves.

A PAUL TO THE THESSALONIANS

Read Acts 17 v 1-10 and 1 Thessalonians 1 v 1

1. Paul, Silvanus (= Silas) and Timothy had all been part of the beginning of the church at Thessalonika. As they write this letter (perhaps only shortly after leaving Thessalonika), what memories do you imagine are flooding through their minds (Acts 17 v 1-10)? Why do they think it's important to say what they do about the church in v 1?

B PAUL'S THANKSGIVING

Read verses 2-3

2. What does Paul give thanks for as he prays for the Thessalonians (v 2-3)?

3. Most of us are poor at thanksgiving. What from this passage will help you to thank God more for your fellow Christians (v 2-3)?

C GOD'S CHOICE OF THE THESSALONIANS

Read verses 4-7

4. What facts make Paul sure that God loves the Thessalonians and has chosen them (v 4-7)?

5. What is the same evidence of God's love for, and choice of, your Bible-reading partner that you can see in him/her (v 4-7)? Encourage him by telling him.

D THE EFFECTS OF THE THESSALONIANS' FAITH

Read verses 7-10

6. What impact did their faith have on other Christians (v 7-10)?

7. What does Paul mention as the best-known aspects of their faith (v 9-10)?

8. Tell your Bible-reading partner about someone whose faith has had a significant impact on you (v 7-10).

E PRAYING TOGETHER

- Give thanks for God's choice of your Bible-reading partner and the evidence of that in his/her life.
- Give thanks for the people whose faith has encouraged and helped you and your Bible-reading partner, especially those whom you mentioned in answer to question 8.

Session 10 A Christian to imitate

Today's passage: 1 Thessalonians 2 v 1-12

In this passage Paul reminds the Thessalonians about his relationship with them while he was with them. First he speaks of the time when he was witnessing to them before they became Christians ("declar[ing] to you the gospel of God": v 2); then he speaks of the time when he was caring for them after they became Christians (when they had become "his children" in the Lord: v 7, 11). He recalls this relationship partly because he is very fond of them (v 8) and partly to give them an example to imitate in their own relationships, with those who were not yet Christians and with each other. Certainly we Christians today are to identify with Paul in this passage and seek to imitate him.

A PAUL THE CHRISTIAN WITNESS

Read verses 1-6

1. What are the positive aspects of his way of witnessing about which Paul reminds the Thessalonians (v 1-6)? Why are they important?

2. What are the negative aspects of some Christian witness which Paul says he avoided (v 1-6)? Why are they disastrous?

3. Which of these truths do you most need to hear for your own Christian witness now (v 1-6)? Why?

B PAUL THE CHRISTIAN PASTOR – THE MOTHER

Read verses 7-8

Note: Some translations of v 7 use the word "nurse" and some "mother". The correct translation is almost certainly "nursing mother".

❹ In what ways is Paul the pastor like a breast-feeding mother (v 7-8)? Why are these qualities important?

C PAUL THE CHRISTIAN PASTOR – THE FATHER

Read verses 9-12

❺ In what ways is Paul the pastor like a father (v 9-12)? Why is that important?

❻ Which are you most like in caring for your fellow Christians: Paul the mother or Paul the father (v 7-12)? What in these verses do you reckon are strengths for you (don't be over-humble; give the glory to God) (v 7-12)?

❼ How in practice can you strengthen those motherly/fatherly aspects in which you are weaker?

D PRAYING TOGETHER

- Give praise for the strengths you see in your Bible-reading partner, in line with question 6.
- Pray for your Bible-reading partner's and your own witness to friends who are not yet Christians, in line with question 3.
- Pray for your Bible-reading partner's and your own caring for other Christians, in line with question 7.

Session 11 Applying as closely as possible

Today's passage: 1 Thessalonians 2 v 13-20

We've already seen that one of the best ways to mine the riches of the epistles is to put yourself into the shoes of the writer or the people written to. Sometimes this is more difficult: the intensity of the Thessalonians' suffering (which may have included murder: v15) is not what you probably experience. But instead of simply skipping over those parts as irrelevant, it means we need to think harder: What is the nearest equivalent in our experience? If we ask that question carefully, God can still speak to us through the passage.

A RECEIVING THE WORD OF GOD

Read verse 13

1. What are the things Paul thanks God for (v 13)? Why are they a cause for praise?

2. Have you seen the same things in yourself or others? When?

B RECEIVING OPPOSITION

Read verses 14-16

3. What sorts of suffering does it seem that the Thessalonians faced (v 14-16)?

4. What does Paul say to encourage them (v 13-16)?

5. The suffering you face will probably not be so intense, but what is the nearest equivalent in your experience of opposition as a Christian (v 14-16)? How can these verses encourage you (v 13-16)?

C RECEIVING A CROWN

Read verses 17-20

6. How does Paul feel about the Thessalonians now (v 17-20)?

7. How will Paul feel about the Thessalonians at the Second Coming (v 19-20)?

8. Who are the people about whom you could say the same things (v 17-20)? Is it for the same reasons as here (v 17-20)?

D PRAYING TOGETHER

- Give thanks to God for what He has done in you or others, in line with your answers to question 2.
- Pray for your Bible-reading partner, in line with their answer to question 5.
- Give thanks for the people who are your "glory and joy" in the Lord (question 8).

Session 12 Worried about their faith

Today's passage: 1 Thessalonians 3 v 1-8

Those of us who are parents worry about the faith of our children, especially when they leave home. Most of us are members of a church; we worry about people who seem to be drifting away from the life of the church. All of us have friends; we worry about the influences on some of our friends which may pull them away from Christ. In this passage, Paul writes about his worries for the Thessalonians' faith.

A FEARS ABOUT THEIR FAITH

Read verses 1-5

1. What facts made Paul worried that the Thessalonians might have lost their faith (v 3-5)? Is it the same things (or different factors) which make us worried about the faith of people we love (v 3-5)?

2. What had Paul done – in the past and more recently – to help them face their problems (v 1-5)?

3. What does this passage teach us about how we can help those we love from faltering in their faith (v 1-5)?

4. Who have you been thinking of as you've read these verses (v 1-5)? Whose faith do you worry about most?

B COMFORT FROM THEIR FAITH

Read verses 6-8

5. What were the different aspects of the Thessalonians' lives that encouraged Paul (v 6-8)?

6. Which of these aspects do you see most clearly in the Christians you love (v 6-8)? Give some examples.

7. What effects does Paul say their faith has on him (v 6-8)? Is he exaggerating? Why (not)?

8. Who have you been thinking of as you've read these verses (v 6-8)? Whose faith gives you most joy?

C PRAYING TOGETHER

- Pray for those people whose faith you or your Bible-reading partner are most worried about. In particular, pray for any appropriate ways to help them which this passage has suggested to you.
- Give praise for those people whose faith gives you most encouragement. In particular, give thanks for those aspects of their life which are also mentioned in this passage.

Session 13 Deepening prayer

Today's passage: 1 Thessalonians 3 v 9-13

Most of us know that our prayer life is rather shallow. We pray for ourselves, and our families and friends, but what we are asking for is probably not what God considers really important. One of the best ways of deepening our prayer lives is to read, and think carefully, about the way biblical men and women prayed and to change our way of praying to be more like theirs.

A PAUL'S LIFE OF PRAYER

Read verses 9-10

1. What aspects of Paul's life of prayer strike you (v 9-10)? Why do you find them striking?

2. What does Paul pray for here (v 9-10)? Why does he consider these things important (v 9-10)?

3. What changes will you make to your prayer life, so as to make it more like Paul's (v 9-10)?

B A PRAYER OF PAUL'S

Read verses 11-13

4. What does Paul pray for that is also part of your regular praying (v 11-13)?

5. What does Paul pray for that is not part of your regular praying (v 11-13)? What steps will you take to change the way you pray, so as to include what Paul considered important (v 11-13)?

6. For whom especially do you want to pray the same things that Paul prayed for the Thessalonians (v 10-13)? Why?

7. Which of Paul's prayer requests do you want your Bible-reading partner especially to pray for you (v 10-13)? Why?

C PRAYING TOGETHER

- If possible, spend longer than usual praying together today.
- Pray for your Bible-reading partner some of what Paul prayed for the Thessalonians, especially remembering what your partner said about question 7.
- Pray for the people your partner mentioned in question 6, learning from Paul how to pray for these people.
- Pray that your own regular prayer life will be different as a result of what you've read and thought about today.

Session 14 **Standing out** from the crowd

Today's passage: 1 Thessalonians 4 v 1-12

Christians ought to be noticeably different. People around us don't ask the question: "What would please God?" Yet we are not only to think about that constantly but to live that way (v 2). Our sexual behaviour and fantasies are probably what mark us out most clearly from those who are not yet Christians (v 3-5). The word "holiness" dominates the central section of our passage (v 3, 4, 7); its basic biblical meaning is: set apart. "Outsiders" see our different way of life (v 12). But how are we to be different?

A PLEASING GOD MORE

Read verses 1-2

1. In what ways is your life more pleasing to God now than before you became a Christian (v 1-2)?

2. In what ways does your life need to change, to be still more pleasing to God (v 1-2)?

B SEXUAL PURITY

Read verses 3-8

3. What must you steer clear of to remain sexually pure (v 3-5)?

4. What positive steps must we take to "gain possession of" our own body sexually (v 4-5)? (Note: "Control his own body" appears in some translations as "take a wife for himself". The Greek is literally: "possess his own vessel". This probably means: "gain possession of his own body", particularly its sexual urges.)

5. What reasons does Paul give for accepting that any sexual activity outside marriage is wrong (v 6-8)?

6. Which of these reasons will keep you most from sexual sin (v 6-8)? Why?

C CHRISTIAN LOVE (AND MORE)

Read verses 9-12

7. In what specific ways could you grow in love for other Christians (v 9-10)?

8. Paul finishes this section with some other instructions. Which is most important for you, and why (v 11-12)?

D PRAYING TOGETHER

- Praise God for the ways in which your Bible-reading partner's life does clearly please God and is different from the life of those who are not yet Christians.
- Pray for each other for holiness, especially in your sexual life.
- Pray for each other to grow in love, in line with your answers to question 7.
- Pray for each other to obey what you said was important for you in answer to question 8.

Session 15 Living in the light of the future

Today's passage: 1 Thessalonians 4 v 13 – 5 v 11

Government and businesses are often accused of short-termism: they are only interested in immediate results and can't be bothered with anything which will not bring results for several years. We Christians too often live in the present (and the past!) and rarely look more than a few months ahead. However, the worldview of the New Testament is dominated by the future.

A THE COMING OF THE LORD

Read 4 v 13-18

1. Christians often feel we ought to say: We don't grieve over a believer who has died because (s)he is already in heaven. Is that what Paul says (v 13-18)? If not, what does he say about our grieving (v 13-18)?

2. What does Paul say will happen at "the coming of the Lord" (v 13-17)? What does this tell us about God and His concerns (v 13-17)?

3. In what ways will we "encourage one another" (v 18) by talking together about these truths (v 13-18)?

B THE TIMING OF HIS COMING

Read 5 v 1-3

4. What do we know, and what don't we know, about the coming of the Lord (v 1-3)?

C LIFE IN THE LIGHT OF HIS COMING

Read 5 v 4-8

5. What does Paul say we must avoid to be ready for Christ's coming (v 4-7)? What will it mean in practice for us to avoid those things (v 4-7)?

6. What does Paul say we must do to be ready for Christ's coming (v 5-8)? What will these things mean in practice for us (v 5-8)?

D OUR FUTURE

Read 5 v 9-11

7. Which part of the future that Paul describes here most excites you (v 9-10)? Why?

8. In what ways will we "build one another up" (v 11) by talking together about these truths (v 1-11)?

E PRAYING TOGETHER

- Ask Christ's forgiveness that His coming has so little influence on your thinking and action.
- Give thanks for what Christ will do for Christians you loved who have now died.
- Pray about your own death and how you will face it (if it happens before Christ's coming).
- Give thanks for specific ways in which you have encouraged one another as you have talked about this passage.

Session 16 Don't blink or you'll miss them

Today's passage: 1 Thessalonians 5 v 12-28

The last section of Paul's letters is often rather quickfire. It's easy to skip quickly over this part; but if we do, we'll miss some gems and the opportunity for God to speak to us very practically. If you read verses like these on your own (for example in your daily reading of the Bible), slow down, take a notebook and write down those commands or encouragements which particularly strike you. In your Bible-reading partnership, take the time to discuss these verses fully.

If necessary, leave out questions 7 and 8.

A RELATIONSHIPS IN THE FAMILY OF CHRIST

Read verses 12-15

1. How does Paul say we are to treat our church leaders (v 12-13)?

2. What in practice could you do to put this teaching into effect (v 12-13)?

3. Which of the exhortations in v 14-15 do you most need to hear? Why?

B SHORT, SHARP AND TO THE POINT

Read verses 16-28

4. These final verses have many things to say about how we relate to God. Which are the most important for you to think about and obey – and why (v 16-28)?

5. These final verses have some things to say about how God relates to us. Which are the most important for you to think about and rejoice in – and why (v 16-28)?

6. These final verses have some things to say about how we relate to each other. Which are the most important for you to think about and act on – and why (v 16-28)?

C LOOK BACK IN GRATITUDE

Skim read 1 Thessalonians

7. Which of these 8 studies has changed your thinking most – and how (1 Thessalonians)?

8. Which of these 8 studies has changed your action most – and how (1 Thessalonians)?

D PRAYING TOGETHER

- Give thanks for specific church leaders and pray for them.
- Pray for your relationship with God, in line with your answers to questions 4 and 5.
- Pray for your relationship with other Christians, in line with your answers to questions 3 and 6.
- Thank God for how you have been changed by Paul's writing in 1 Thessalonians.

Review sheet | 1 Thessalonians

The purposes of this review sheet are:
- to help you evaluate your times together
- to make any changes in these times that would make them more helpful
- to consolidate the lessons God has taught you

Discuss your review with your Bible-reading partner when you next meet.

If there is someone in your church in charge of Bible-reading partnerships, make a photocopy of this review and send or give this copy to him/her.

- *How frequently have you normally met?*

  Weekly ❑ Every other week ❑ Once a month ❑ Other ❑

- *Do you want to meet more frequently?*

- *How long did you normally spend?*

Altogether ________ mins In Bible study ________ mins
In prayer ________ mins In general talking ________ mins

- *Do you want to change the balance of your time together?*

- *Which sessions on 1 Thessalonians did you find most helpful? Why?*

- *In what ways, if any, have you changed (in your understanding, praying or acting) as a result of studying 1 Thessalonians together?*

- *1 Thessalonians was written to a church. What are the most important lessons for your church in what you have read? How in practice could you help these lessons for your church become a reality?*

Genesis 1-12

The beginning that shapes the people we are

Session 17 In the beginning, God

Today's passage: Genesis 1 v 1 – 2 v 3

Whatever your view on the creation and evolution question, the Genesis creation chapters give us a theologically accurate and penetrating revelation of God, His activity, and the world He has put us in (though, as the next chapters will show, this "very good" world has been partially spoiled). What Genesis is seeking to tell us needs to be taken with the utmost seriousness.

A THE INTRODUCTION

Read 1 v 1-2

1. What does the introduction tell us about God the Father and God the Spirit (v 1-2)?

   (Note: Verse 2 is not saying that a formless earth existed before God began to create. Rather, God originally created (1) a formless earth and then (2) began to shape/order it. Compare Psalm 139 v 13-16.)

2. Why does the writer tell us these facts about God the Father, God the Spirit and the earth; what response are they to evoke in us (v 1-2)?

B THE FIRST FIVE DAYS

Read 1 v 3-23

3. What do these verses tell us about God (v 3-23)? Which verses show most clearly what you are noticing?

4. What do these verses tell us about the world we live in (v 3-23)?

5 Is there any significance in the order (what comes first, what next, etc.) of God's creating (v 3-23)? If so, what is the significance?

C THE SIXTH DAY

Read 1 v 24-31

6 Why doesn't the creation of humans have a day to itself (v 24-31)?

7 When compared with other creatures, what is the same, and what is different about humans (v 24-31)? What do these differences mean (v 24-31)?

8 What commands does God give humans (v 26-30)?
How can we obey these commands today (v 26-30)?

D THE SEVENTH DAY

Read 2 v 1-3

9 What does the seventh day tell us about God (2 v 1-3)?
What response are we to make to these truths (2 v 1-3)?

E PRAYING TOGETHER

- Give thanks for what you have understood about God the Father and God the Spirit.
- Give thanks for what you have learned about God's world.
- Pray that you will, in your life this coming week, respond appropriately and obediently to what you have learned, in line with your answers to questions 2, 8 and 9.

Session 18 Men and women

Today's passage: **Genesis 2 v 4-25**

Even in a perfect environment, with God very close (see 3 v 8), human beings can be lonely. These verses, with great simplicity and power, show that God understands our loneliness and provides for it. While the rest of the Old Testament shows that friends can meet that need, and the New Testament is revolutionary in its honouring of singleness (see especially 1 Corinthians 7 v 32-35), God's normal provision for loneliness is marriage. Verse 24 is frequently quoted in the New Testament and is the fundamental building-block for a Christian understanding of marriage.

If you are short of time, discuss questions 1 and 5-8; skip questions 2-4.

A THE CREATION OF MAN

Read verses 4-14

1. What do these verses tell us about the Lord God (v 4-14)?

2. What do these verses tell us about human beings (v 5-9)? If we grasp these truths fully, how will they change us (v 5-9)?

3. What do these verses tell us about the environment God originally gave to man (v 4-14)? Given that we are no longer in this environment (see 3 v 23-24), how are we to respond to this part of the creation story (v 4-14)?

B THE COMMANDS TO MAN

Read verses 15-17

❹ What does God tell the man to do and not to do? In what ways can we still obey these positive and negative commands?

C THE CREATION OF WOMAN

Read verses 18-25

❺ What do these verses tell us about the relationship between humans and animals (v 18-20)? How should this affect our relationship with our own, and other people's, pets (v 18-20)?

❻ What do these verses tell us about the relationship between men and women?

❼ What do these verses tell us about right relationships in marriage?

❽ If you are married, what part of verse 24 do you most need to hear? Why? If you are single, how does God want you to respond to verses 18-25?

D PRAYING TOGETHER

- Give praise to God for the good marriages you have been influenced by (including, perhaps, your own).
- Give praise to God for what is similar, and what is different, between men and women; and also pray about the tensions these similarities and differences can bring.
- Ask God to help you obey the explicit (v 15-17) and implied (v 18-25) commands He has given you, in line with your answers to Q4 and Q8.

Session 19 The fall

Today's passage: Genesis 3

Biblical truth is often meant to be understood at more than one level. Old Testament prophecy, for example, often has an immediate fulfilment (in, or soon after, the lifetime of the prophet) and a more distant fulfilment (in the life of Christ or the church); we need to hear both. Genesis 3 tells us about a unique event: the first human disobedience that has had catastrophic effects on all of God's creation, including human life, ever since. But it also tells us of daily events: the normal human experience of being tempted and giving in to sin. Again, we need to hear both truths. This study may take you two weeks.

A THE TEMPTATION

Read verses 1-6

1. How did the serpent/tempter show that he was "crafty" (v 1-6)?

2. Why did the woman, and why did her husband, knowingly disobey God (v 1-6)?

3. What of your own experience of temptation do you recognise in this story (v 1-6)? Knowing these truths (v 1-6), what specific, practical steps will you take to overcome temptation?

B THE RESULTS

Read verses 7-13

4. What effects did their sin have on their self-perception (v 7-13)?

5. What effects did their sin have on their relationship with God (v 7-13)?

6. What effects did their sin have on their relationship with each other (v 7-13)?

7. What of the effects of your sin do you recognise in this story (v 7-13)? Knowing these truths (v 7-13), what specific, practical steps will you take to avoid sin?

C THE CURSE

Read verses 14-24

8. Given that the New Testament regards the serpent as the devil (see Revelation 12 v 9; 20 v 2), what do these verses tell us about the state of the devil now?

9. In what ways has God cursed women (v 16, 20)? (Note: To understand verse 16b, see the similar language of 4 v 7b) Why has God chosen these areas of a woman's life to curse (v 16, 20)?

10. In what ways has God cursed men (v 17-19)? Why has God chosen these areas of a man's life to curse (v 17-19)?

11. In what other ways does God respond to human sin (v 21-24)?

12. In what ways do you experience these curses on the first couple's sin in your daily life (v 14-24)? How does the writer of Genesis want us to respond to these verses (v 14-24)?

D PRAYING TOGETHER

- Confess to God your solidarity in the first couple's disobedience and sin.
- Cry to God for His help in your battle against temptations.
- Acknowledge humbly before God that He is right to bring His curse/ judgment on sin.
- Thank God that in Jesus' death He has shouldered and removed your sin.

Session 20 Anger in the family

Today's passage: Genesis 4 v 1-16

In this story also the Bible speaks to us at two levels. Certainly it is a story about anger and its consequences. We, as sinful human beings, can identify with this, even if we don't commit actual murder (see Matthew 5 v 21-26). But the writer of Genesis is also wanting to tell us something about the early story of human beings on earth and the world they shaped, which we now live in.

A THE OVERALL PICTURE

Read verses 1-16

1. Why does the writer of Genesis tell this story?

B THE ANGER

Read verses 1-8

2. What was it that made Cain so upset (v 1-8)?

3. Are you angry with any member of your family?
   If so, is it at all for the same reasons you see in these verses (v 1-8)?

4. What does God's reply tell us about Himself and about Cain (v 6-7)?

5. How does Cain respond to God's warning (v 6-8)? In what circumstances have you responded to God's warnings in the same way (v 6-8)?

C GOD'S RESPONSE

Read verses 9-16

6. Why does God keep asking questions when He knows people have sinned (v 9-10; compare 3 v 9, 11, 13)? Have you found yourself being questioned by God after you have sinned? If so, how?

7. In what ways is God's curse after Cain's sin different from His curse after Adam's sin (v 10-14; compare 3 v 17-19)?

8. What else does God say and do (v 15-16)? What does God's whole response (v 9-16) tell us about God?

9. Cain "went away from the presence of the Lord" (v 16) despite God's mercy. Do our sins have the same consequences for us? Why /why not?

D PRAYING TOGETHER

- Pray together about any anger you feel, especially towards members of your family; ask God's help to "rule over it" (v 7).
- Ask God to stop the rot of sin growing in your life and in your community.
- Thank God for His mercy towards you, even though you may have to live with some of the consequences of your sin.

Session 21 Noah and judgment

Today's passage: Genesis 6 v 5 – 7 v 24

Children are given a Noah's Ark as a toy. Our church parents and toddlers group is called Noah's Ark. It's a colourful and charming story. Or is it? A closer look reveals it as a story of appalling human sin, God's terrible judgment and His great mercy. We must not shrink from thinking seriously about each of these truths.

A HUMAN SIN

Read 6 v 5-12

1. What do these verses say about human sin, and God's reaction to it, in Noah's day (6 v 5-12)?

2. In what ways was Noah different (6 v 8-9)?

3. To what extent can we say the same about human sin, and God's reaction, today (6 v 5-12)? What makes you say that?

B GOD'S RESPONSE

Read 6 v 13 – 7 v 4

4. What is God's response to human sin (6 v 13 – 7 v 4)? Is this an over-reaction (6 v 13 – 7 v 4)? Why (not)?

5 What is God's response to Noah and some animals (6 v 13 – 7 v 4)?

6 The New Testament sees what God did for Noah as a picture of Christ's rescue of us (see 1 Peter 3 v 20-21; 2 Peter 2 v 4-10). What similarities do you see between God's rescue of Noah and Christ's rescue of us (6 v 13 – 7 v 4; 1 Peter 3 v 20-21; 2 Peter 2 v 4-10)?

C NOAH'S OBEDIENCE

Read 7 v 5-9

7 Noah "did all that the Lord had commanded him" (7 v 5-9; compare 6 v 22). How can we "do all that the Lord commands us" in relation to His rescue of us (read also Hebrews 11 v 7)?

D GOD'S JUDGMENT

Read 7 v 10-24

8 In what ways did God react to the world of Noah's day (7 v 10-24)?

9 In what ways will God react to the people of our day (7 v 10-24; read also Matthew 24 v 37-51)?

10 Can we feel comfortable about God's judgment? Why/why not?

E PRAYING TOGETHER

- Bow in humility before God, acknowledging the justice of His judgements.
- Bow in gratitude before God, thanking Him for His mercy to you.
- Bow in urgent prayer before God, asking Him to bring to repentance and faith to those who are not Christians whom you love.

Session 22 Noah and mercy

Today's passage: Genesis 8 v 1 – 9 v 17

Once more this biblical story speaks to us at two levels. It is the story of God's commitment to continuing life and fruitfulness on earth; and it is a picture of God's commitment to us because of the death and resurrection of Christ.

Questions 6-8 are the most important; make sure you have time to discuss them.

A GOD'S JUDGMENT WITHDRAWN

Read 8 v 1-14

1. What did God do to remove His judgement from the earth (8 v 1-5)?

2. How did Noah confirm that God's judgment had been removed (8 v 6-14)?

3. What gradually increasing signs do we have which confirm that God has removed His judgment from us?

B A NEW BEGINNING

Read 8 v 15-20

4. What did God tell Noah to do, and what did Noah do, to show that a new era of mercy had dawned (8 v 15-20)?

5. What equivalent actions can we take, to show our awareness that God's mercy in Christ has come (8 v 15-20)?

C GOD'S PROMISES

Read 8 v 21 – 9 v 17

6. What does God promise Noah and "all future generations" (8 v 21 – 9 v 17)?

7. How can we be sure God will not revoke these promises (8 v 21 – 9 v 17)?

8. What do you most need to hear in what these verses tell us about God and about us (8 v 21 – 9 v 17)? Why?

D PRAYING TOGETHER

- Give praise to God that, despite human sinfulness (8 v 21), He will never again destroy the earth (until the earth's transformation on the Last Day).
- Give praise to God for His mercy in Christ and His covenant with you.
- Give praise to God for what you have seen of His character in the entire Noah story (6 v 5 – 9 v 17).

Session 23 Work and community sin

Today's passage: Genesis 11 v 1-9

We tend to be individualistic as Christians: we read the Bible as if it was all about each individual and his or her relationship with God. But it isn't. Large parts of the Bible are about a corporate relationship with God: how our family relates to God, or our nation, or our community, or our church—or our business. We also tend to be blind to what the Bible says about work; we think of it as only applying to our life away from work. This is one of many Bible passages which speak of work and/or community life.

A HUMAN ENDEAVOUR

Read verses 1-4

1. What did the people try to do (v 1-4)?

2. Why did they try to do it (v 1-4)?

3. In the light of God's reaction (v 5-9), what was wrong in what they did (v 1-4)?

4. Does that mean that the rest of what they did was good or neutral (v 1-4)? How do you know?

5. Are there things which are wrong about the way you work or about your community involvement (v 1-4)?

B DIVINE JUDGMENT

Read verses 5-9

6. What does God do to them, as His judgment on them (v 5-9)?

7. Why does God do it (v 5-9)?

8. In the light of this passage, what aspects of community or international relations are a result of God's judgment (v 1-9)?

9. Taking this passage with Genesis 2 v 5, 8, 15, what does Genesis 1 – 11 teach you about how to do your specific work and how not to do it?

C PRAYING TOGETHER

- Ask God to help you think more biblically: to see yourself in solidarity with your family, community, workforce, nation and church.
- Confess the ways in which the mindset and practices of your place of work are contrary to God's will, and ask Him for the courage to change these ways.
- Confess the ways in which the people you associate with turn you and themselves away from God, and ask Him for the wisdom to know how to change these ways.
- Confess the ways in which (y)our nation is proudly independent and ask God to make you/us more humble/dependent on Him.

Session 24 God blesses one man and the world

Today's passage: Genesis 11 v 27 – 12 v 7

God sees us, and deals with us, both as individuals and as members of the various communities we belong to (see Session 23). His answer to community sin is frequently an individual; his dealings with that individual have implications for the whole community the individual leads and represents. That is exactly what God does in Abraham, the father of the Jewish nation. It is also what God does in His Son, Jesus Christ.

A THE CHARACTERS

Read 11 v 27-32

1. What does the writer want us to know about Abram, about his family and his family's plans (11 v 27-32)?
   Why does he want us to know this (11 v 27-32)?

B THE BLESSING

Read 12 v 1-3

2. What does God tell Abram to do (12 v 1)?
   Why was this difficult?

3. What does God promise to do for Abram (12 v 1-3)?

4. How will the promise to Abram affect other people (12 v 2-3)?

5. The New Testament speaks of close links between what God promised Abraham and what He does for us in Christ (see especially Galatians 3 v 7-9, 16). In what ways is God's promise to Abram like, and/or fulfilled in what He does in Christ (12 v 1-3)?

C THE ARRIVAL

Read 12 v 4-7

6. How does Abram respond to what God has said (12 v 4-7)?
   What are the equivalent ways in which you need to respond (12 v 4-7)?

7. What does Abram find, and experience, in Canaan (12:5b-7)?

8. In what ways is this passage a turning point in the book of Genesis so far (11 v 27 – 12 v 7 in the light of chapters 1-11)?
   What does this turning point tell us about God (11 v 27 – 12 v 7)?

D PRAYING TOGETHER

- Thank God for His extraordinary mercy in the face of our, and our community's, sin.
- Thank God for the way He blessed the Jewish people and continues to bless "all the families of the earth".
- Pray for your response to God's mercy, in line with your answers to question 6.
- Pray about whether your Bible-reading partner and you should now each take on a new partner for Bible reading and so multiply this ministry (see 'Where do we go from here?', page 61).

Review sheet | Genesis 1-12

The purposes of this review sheet are:
- to help you evaluate your times together
- to make any changes in these times that would make them more helpful
- to consolidate the lessons God has taught you

Discuss your review with your Bible-reading partner when you next meet.

If there is someone in your church in charge of Bible-reading partnerships, make a photocopy of this review and send or give this copy to him/her.

- *How frequently have you normally met?*

Weekly ❑ Every other week ❑ Once a month ❑ Other ❑

- *Do you want to meet more frequently?*

- *How long did you normally spend?*

Altogether _________ mins In Bible study _________ mins
In prayer _________ mins In general talking _________ mins

- *Do you want to change the balance of your time together?*

- *Which sessions on Genesis 1 – 12 did you find most helpful? Why?*

- *In what ways, if any, has your understanding of God, or of yourself, or of your solidarity with other human groupings, changed as a result of reading Genesis 1-12?*

- *In what ways has your partner helped you as you have read the Bible and prayed together?*

Where do we go from here?

- Our hope is that an increasing number of Christians will be involved in, and benefit from, Bible-reading partnerships. If you have enjoyed and gained from the partnership which has just finished, we imagine that you share that hope.

- If so, you can help to fulfil this vision. Rather than staying with the same Bible-reading partner—which would be comfortable but would not spread the benefits of Bible partnerships—choose a new Bible-reading partner of your own sex and start again.

- In this new partnership, you can be the more experienced Christian and share with someone who will gain from being your partner.

- You may think that it will be dull going over the same material. Experience shows that it will be a totally new experience. The Bible itself doesn't change, but your new Bible-reading partner will bring different insights, and you will have moved on as well. We recommend that you obtain a new copy of this book and write down your answers to the questions afresh. This will ensure that you continue to gain new insights.

- Alternatively, you can order *One2One Book One* (24 studies in John 13-17, Philippians and Psalms), published by the Good Book Company. Both books are at about the same level.

- You will need to be willing to change down a few gears. You probably remember that your present partnership took some weeks to get going. You must expect the same with your new partnership. It may be a little sticky at first but you will gradually grow in friendship and mutual trust. A new and equally valuable partnership will blossom little by little.

- Not everyone, of course, will want to begin a new partnership; some will want to take a break, at least for a while. But we hope that you will be willing to begin in the near future with a new partner and discover all over again the value of *ONE2ONE*.

Where do we go from here?

- Do you want to start again with a new Bible-reading partner? YES / NO
- If so, when would you like to start? ____________________
- Who would you invite to be your next Bible-reading partner (perhaps a less experienced Christian of your own sex)?
  ____
- If there is someone in your church in charge of Bible-reading partnerships, please be in touch with them to let them know that you are starting a new partnership or to ask their help in suggesting someone suitable to be your next partner.

More Bible study resources for you, your church and your family

Explore

Many Christians find it difficult to adopt a pattern of regular Bible study and prayer. That's where *Explore* can help! Each issue features three months of daily readings to help you understand and apply the message and challenge of God's word.

Our introductory edition of *Explore* is called *Time with God*, and it's designed to help Christians develop the discipline of a regular quiet time. It uses the same format as *Explore*, contains 28 studies and is the perfect way to kick-start your quiet times.

Table Talk

Many parents struggle to read the Bible consistently with their children — but help is at hand. *Table Talk* is designed to form the basis for a short family Bible time — maybe just five minutes at breakfast or dinner. It includes a simple discussion starter or activity that leads into a short Bible reading and some ideas for prayer.

Good Book Guides

Good Book Guides seek to uncover the meaning of a passage and see how it fits into the big picture of the Bible while leading people to apply what they have learned to their lives. *Good Book Guides* are ideal for small groups or individual study.

UK & Europe: www.thegoodbook.co.uk
N America: www.thegoodbook.com
Australia: www.thegoodbook.com.au
New Zealand: www.thegoodbook.co.nz

At The Good Book Company, we are dedicated to helping Christians and local churches grow. We believe that God's growth process always starts with hearing clearly what He has said to us through His timeless word—the Bible.

Ever since we opened our doors in 1991, we have been striving to produce resources that honour God in the way the Bible is used. We have grown to become an international provider of user-friendly resources to the Christian community, with believers of all backgrounds and denominations using our Bible studies, books, evangelistic resources, DVD-based courses and training events.

We want to equip ordinary Christians to live for Christ day by day, and churches to grow in their knowledge of God, their love for one another, and the effectiveness of their outreach. Call us for a discussion of your needs, or visit one of our websites for more information on the resources and services we provide, and how to obtain our materials throughout the world.

UK & Europe: www.thegoodbook.co.uk

N America: www.thegoodbook.com

Australia: www.thegoodbook.com.au

New Zealand: www.thegoodbook.co.nz

Tel UK: 0845 225 0880

Tel International: +44 (0) 208 942 0880

Also available in the One2One series...
One2One Book One

Don't miss Andrew Cornes' first One2One study guide featuring:

- 24 studies on John, Philippians and Psalms for Bible-reading partnerships
- Review sheets to help evaluate your time with your Bible-reading partner